BITS AND PIECES

A Roaming

by

EDWARD POMERANTZ

Ben Yehuda Press
Teaneck, New Jersey

Published by Ben Yehuda Press
122 Ayers Court #1B
Teaneck, NJ 07666

http://www.BenYehudaPress.com

To subscribe to our monthly book club and support independent Jewish publishing, visit https://www.patreon.com/BenYehudaPress

Jewish Poetry Project #37   http://jpoetry.us

Ben Yehuda Press books may be purchased at a discount by synagogues, book clubs, and other institutions buying in bulk. For information, please email markets@BenYehudaPress.com

ISBN13 978-1-953829-56-6

24 25 26 / 10 9 8 7 6 5 4 3 2   20240101

for

*Eddie G
and
Gert and Al*

1

I am my father's son.
Same dome. Same cock.
His hands—boning a shad,
removing its thousands of bones with knife and tweezer.
Mine—working with words,
telling a story,
removing the fat.

2

A movie with a stage show.
You take the downtown A.
A ride like no other.
Where you get to see colored people
at the two stops they get on at.
Where after 125th you get a thrill speeding up,
all the stops flashing by,
all the way to 59th.

You're 7. 8. 10.
The stage show is The Rockettes. Sinatra. Swing and Sway
with Sammy Kaye.
At the Music Hall. Paramount. Strand.
For only 55 cents (before 1 o'clock),
with a cartoon, a newsreel, a March of Time, coming attractions.

This is it.
Where it happens.

Bette Davis, still, on the sofa, without blinking, her husband begging for
his medicine, struggling to breathe, collapsing and dying on the stairs.

Barbara Stanwyck, legs crossed, high heels with pompoms. Her husband
isn't home. She's alone with Fred MacMurray. Eyes listening with a smile
while he sells her insurance, admires her anklet.

Ronald Reagan, legs broken in a train accident, unconscious, on the
operating table. The doctor hates Reagan. His daughter's in love with
him. He decides to amputate. Without chloroform.

Fuck Bambi. Betty Grable. Andy Hardy.

This is where the truth, where danger is.
This is where you want to live for the rest of your life.

Edward Pomerantz

3

He's your cousin.
But when you're together and you meet people,
they take you for brothers.
Twins.
Your mothers are sisters.
Pregnant together.
He comes first.
Then you, six weeks later.
Both named for Esther.
Our mothers' mother.
He's Edwin.
You're Edward.
But when people ask you your names, you tell them
Eddie.
Both of you.
Together.
Eddie.
Twin Eddies.
The one from Weehawken.
The one from Washington Heights.
Together
every weekend.
Every summer
in the same house
in Rockaway,
days together
on the boardwalk,
in the ocean,
at the penny arcade,
on the hot burning sand.

Laughing.
Always laughing,
And eating.
Always eating.
Both round.
Roly-polies
from our mothers' cooking
and Yankee Doodles
and Good Humors
and Dr. Brown's cream soda
and Chinese egg rolls.
Our childhood free
and fun
through all our terrors—
polio,
disappearing sandbars,
cramps that would drown us,
crabs biting our feet,
while our families did card tricks
and told dirty jokes,
played Gin and Canasta,
watched Milton Berle.
The twin Eddies!
Can't tell one from the other
on our twin Schwinns,
pedaling fast,
no hands.

But then one Eddie dies.
37. In his car. Alone. On the shoulder of a parkway.
Where he's pulled over. With a pain in his chest.

Edward Pomerantz

And when you get the call in Santa Monica,
the Eddie you've become
becomes the Eddie you were,
when you were Eddies in Rockaway,
and you say no,
no, you won't be flying home
for the funeral,
because if the plane crashes
there'll be no Eddies,
and you have to stay alive
for the dead Eddie,
live forever,
if you have to.

4

"I must be dying."
Of course.
The children have called you.
Why else would you be here?
Catch a flight.
Show up out of nowhere.
"I have a book for you," you tell her.
"I came to read it to you."
She's your Aunt May.
Your father's sister.
The baby in the family.
The last of all of them,
all seven,
all gone now,
in her early 80s,
dying ageless
without a wrinkle,
hair undone from its bun
shook free
down her back.
Aunt May.
The Bohemian
dancing in her Capezios,
married to the Gentile,
your Uncle Jimmy,
who drinks scotch all day
starting with breakfast,
ashamed of being German
for murdering the Jews.
It's to May's house you go
for Jimmy to teach you chess,
and dance to Tchaikovsky,
and learn to eat raw hamburger,
raw egg on top,

read *PM*,
the Commie paper,
no Dick Tracy.
It's May you take fast walks with
talking all the way.
May, you send books to,
bring Grace Paley
when she's days away from dying.
An Interest In Life.
She likes the title.
Listens with her eyes closed.
You don't know she's fallen asleep
until she wakes and sees you.
"You're still here," she says.
Then in surprise and wonder,
"And I'm still here,"
and we laugh,
and finish the story.

5

Your Aunt Doris.
Married to Uncle Abe
Your father's oldest brother.
Aunt Doris.
Singing.
On a lake,
you rowing,
on pitch with the birds.
Aunt Doris.
Sobbing.
When she comes to your house the night Amy dies.
Amy.
Her only child,
her daughter,
13,
killed by polio,
freed from the iron lung.
Aunt Doris.
Who twice a year has to go
to the hospital
for shock treatments
when she stands at her closet
and can't make up her mind
which dress to put on,
which shoes.
Aunt Doris.
Who reminds you of all those character actresses in movies
you've seen a million times and don't know their names.
The ones who play the small town neighbor,
storekeeper,
wife of the minister, mayor.
Nice. Friendly. Kind.
Not a mean bone in her body.
Aunt Doris.

Edward Pomerantz

Who you haven't thought of in years
and comes back to you singing,
sobbing,
sitting in silence after shock treatments
looking sad,
like she's lost something,
if she could just remember where she's put it,
what it is.

6

Never saw anything like it.
In the movies.
On a stage.
In real life.
Your mother
getting the news,
your father telling her
right after the call,
no warning,
just Beatie's dead.
Beatie.
Her sister.
Protector.
When their mother died
and deserted them,
left them alone
with their father.
Beatie dead.
48.
The cancer a secret.
Beatie dead.
Bang!
And what you've never seen
before or since
is someone
falling,
backwards,
hitting the living-room floor,
straight as an ironing board.

Edward Pomerantz

7

He's a famous author.
Wrote a book they turned into a movie that won an Oscar.
You're 19.
He's read your play.
Comes to your house for dinner.
Your parents feeding him
like he's one of us.
Family.
Shtupping him
with roast chicken, fish, noodles with pot cheese.
This famous author.
Who wrote a book they turned into a movie that won an Oscar.
Here!
Sitting in our kitchen.
On Pinehurst Avenue.
Three and a half rooms.
65 dollars a month.
Yours, the half-room
with the roll-top desk
that takes up most of it,
a bed that just makes it,
a view of the alley.

Now it's your turn.
To go to his place.
His pad in the city
when he's not with his wife and daughters in Connecticut.
A converted maids quarters in the Dakota,
a castle on the park,
where he tells you Katharine Hepburn sat in the chair you're in
and invites you upstairs to meet a famous playwright.

This is the moment.
When you learn something.
When upstairs,

on a red velvet bordello sofa,
the famous playwright,
eye-shadowed and rouged,
in a room bigger than a thousand of your rooms,
is with his Boy Toy for the evening,
and you know he thinks you're the famous author's Boy Toy,
which, you're not sure why, you enjoy letting him think.
You enjoy his thinking he knows the truth.
And what you learn in that moment is
the truth doesn't give a fuck
what anybody thinks.
The truth is what you know.
What nobody can take from you.
Your silent best friend.
Your bullet-proof vest.

8

You're on a crosstown bus
when it hits you.
Not like a thunderbolt
or a ton of bricks.
More like the sky opening
when you drive cross country
and hit Nebraska.
And not like a thunderstorm
or crack of lightning.
Quiet.
Like a hush
or trickle
or sound in the woods.
Your parents are dead.
But shhh.
Wait.
You don't have to go with them.

9

Sung to the Melody of Hatikvah

"When I was single I had nothing to do.
I sat by my window lacing up my shoe.
Then I got married
I had so much to do
I had so many children
I didn't know what to do.
One cried "Mama, put me into bed."
Another cried "Papa, gimme a piece of bread."
Mama!
Papa!
All day long they cry to you.
Now they are married
I don't know what to do."

This is the lullaby my mother sang.
To me.
Which explains everything.

Edward Pomerantz

10

Second cousin Sadie has a sister Crazy Yetta
who sits at the window all day
and watches us play stickball
and salugi
and Johnny-Ride-A-Pony
across the street
where the crazy lady
on the third floor
shakes out a bottle of Clorox on us,
which is why we play there
right under her window,
to drive the crazy lady crazier,
Crazy Yetta our audience.

11

A vaudeville act.
Uncle Edgar, the ventriloquist,
your Aunt Sarah and their son Donald
his Charlie McCarthys,
rehearsed and waiting for you
since your last visit,
to do it all over again,
entertain you,
make you glad you came,
want to come back.

Donald is a hydrocephalic.
A water-head.
With too much water in his brain,
he was supposed to die when he was born,
but he's older than you are,
a teenager now,
and even though his head is huge
and his body and hands all twisted,
he's happy
and even handsome.
A young FDR
with a Frankenstein forehead.

Just pretend he's normal,
your mother reminds you.

His head is big because he's got more brains than anybody,
Uncle Edgar tells us.

Aunt Sarah doesn't see Donald's big head.
She knits him caps any growing boy would wear.

Aunt Sarah was once a great beauty.

Edward Pomerantz

In the old photograph album, she looks like a silent-movie star.
She was once a lot of things.
A fashion designer.
A buyer for Saks.
A woman ahead of her time.

Until she met Edgar and he put his spell on her,
your mother says in the car going home.
He doesn't let her breathe, think, make a move without him.

Uncle Edgar looks like Woodrow Wilson.
He smiles a lot,
and scares the shit out of you.

The visits are twice a year.
Like two-a-days
in vaudeville,
a repeat performance.
Donald,
doing his Jack Benny,
excited by our laughter,
rocking up and down,
Aunt Sarah,
whooping,
so happy we're here again
making her beautiful Donald so happy,

Uncle Edgar,
so proud
of his big-brained
bouncing
boffo
baby boy.

12

1B.
The center of the universe.
Our apartment in the Heights.

This is where they all come.
The hub.
Gert and Al's place.
The door always open.
A cast of thousands
in our square-boxed stage-set living-room,
side-show kitchen.

All the women in the building
and from blocks around.
Mildred and Jeanette and Ida and Estelle,
and Shirley and Irene and Selma and Evelyn,
in and out,
re-entering,
in different hairdos and dye jobs,
changing costumes—
house dresses,
snoods,
bare midriffs,
fox stoles,
Persian lambs,
bedroom slippers,
open-toed wedges.

They come to play.
Mah Jong and cards.
They come for the laughs,
the jokes about husbands,
Gert's coffee and cake,
her command of the table.

One bam!
Two crack!
Three clubs!
Four aces!
Gert sets the pace,
keeps the whip snapping.

All your friends come too.
For Al's show.
After school
when Al's home from work—
getting up at four in the morning
to bone shad in the Fulton Fish Market,
bone shad all day
in famous seafood restaurants
all over the city,
in Brooklyn,
til four in the afternoon
when nobody's father but yours is home,
sitting in a tub soaking the stink of fish out,
reigning in his orange velvet easy chair,
greeting Howie and Lewie
in his terry wrap loin cloth,
a whale-bellied Tarzan
with lobster red feet,
no extra charge
when he crosses his legs,
and you can see his balls.

They come for Al's stories.
When he was a kid in knickers,
rode the backs of trolley cars,
called his house full of brothers and sisters,
"Hello, Ma! Al!"
"Wait," she says. "I'll see if he's home."
Al's days as a model

Bits and Pieces

when he had a great physique,
posing naked.
His buddy Nosebleed.
A gusher!
Every girl!
Everytime!
Just when he's about to pop!
The shad.
A fish you couldn't eat
without choking on the bones,
little needles,
a hundred to a mouthful,
til he had one x-rayed by a doctor,
and figured it out—
every bone gone
with just a knife and tweezer,
in the beginning one an hour,
now one a minute,
his nails filed and manicured,
fingers fast and light.

1B.
Where after the war
the friends who got rich and moved away come.
In their Buicks and minks
with their nose jobs and ulcers.

From Great Neck.
Riverdale.
Up from Florida when it gets hot there.
The women leather skinned,
golfers, in real estate, alcoholics.
The men all tanned and brilliantined,
patting bellies, tugging at crotches.
They can't stay away,
says Al when they leave again.

Edward Pomerantz

1B's got Gert's brisket.
And the Heights are where the breeze is.

The breeze.
And the brisket.
Intermingled forever
with the laughter and stories,
the clicking of Mah Jong tiles,
the shuffling of cards,
all remembered in the body
to be summoned on deathbeds.

13

When he gets the card he's been waiting for—
the Queen—
to slide between his Jack and King—
he shouts "In the *lambanzo!*"
And when he's dealt Gin, he doesn't say Gin,
he shouts *"Quatalamaylo!"*
Words he's made up
to meet the moment,
rise to the occasion.
You love this man.
This man is your father.
You love him
for inventing a country
where they speak this language,
where words make music
and sing like trumpets.

14

Except for Mister Ostroff,
the boys' shop teacher,
you're educated by women.
All Irish,
All Misses.
Old Maids, they're called,
but except for the Principal,
Miss Regan,
blonde helmeted and built like a tank,
they must have been young then,
some just starting out,
flush with Teacher Power,
Authority,
Control.
What did they teach you,
these young Irish women?
What did you learn from them?
Sitting there at your inkwelled desk
with your hands folded
until they call on you.
What sticks in your brain?
Stays with you?
The Devaney sisters—
Margaret and Catherine—
sneaking smokes at recess.
Miss Costello's lipstick,
a tomato-red smudge where her mouth is,
a powdered face you'll recognize
when you see your first Kabuki.
Miss Flanagan at Open School Week
telling your parents you're her favorite.

Miss Kelly,
who lives in Hudson View Gardens,
where they don't allow Jews.
Miss Donovan, the science teacher,
who, if we promise to behave,
will take time out from Biology
and sing Tit Willow on her stool
with crossed legs,
cupping her breasts.

This is what you remember
of your early education.
When your brain was in the hands
of young unmarried Irish women.

15

He's Johnny McCall.
An Irish kid with a pompadour.
The only kid in school,
in the neighborhood,
who's not Jewish.
Who calls you Eddie Ants-In-His-Pants
and has a big bulge where his fly is.

16

You're supposed to welcome them.
Make them feel at home.
Put it all behind them.
The German refugees.
Fleeing the Nazis.
Moving in.
More and more now.
The Fischels.
And the Werthheimers.
The Goldfarbs.
The Strausses.
Forced to give up their country houses,
maids and governesses,
furs,
tutors,
pianos,
diamonds.
You try to like them,
make friends, good neighbors,
but Mrs. Fischel treats your mother like dirt,
and Mr. Werthheimer has that look—like his shit doesn't smell,
and every day in the schoolyard,
Freddie Strauss likes to push you around,
start a fight,
make fun of you,
for no reason at all.
Little Hitler,
your mother calls him.

Edward Pomerantz

17

He's your rich uncle.
The only relative who doesn't live in the Bronx
or New Jersey.
Uncle Ben.
Your mother's older brother.
Who lives in Phoenix
with a Society Page wife,
no children,
a dog,
a swimming pool.
A self-made man,
they call him.
Left home at sixteen,
landed in Cuba,
made a fortune and lost it
still in his twenties.
This is the legend,
the lore you grow up with.
The Rich Uncle.
The Man Who Made Himself.
Who comes to New York
twice a year
on business,
your mother and her sister
in combat,
outdoing each other
with his favorites—
the brisket and kugels,
macaroons and rugelach
their sainted mother made.

Uncle Ben.
You and your cousin at his side
at the head of the table,

his chubby young princes,
his pants high above a mound of belly,
belt at his chest,
an elephant with pockets.
Uncle Ben.
Made of money.
Sends you bikes and baseball mitts,
makes sure you go to college.
Pays the rent for a year
when your father gets sick
with rheumatoid arthritis,
sits only front row center
at a Broadway show,
where second cousin Sadie says she saw him
with what she's sure was a call girl,
and your mother calls Sadie's mouth a toilet,
never speaks to her again.
Uncle Ben.
Fed and worshipped by sisters,
politely thank-you'd by nephews
who kick each other under the table
secretly laughing at his pachyderm balls.
Uncle Ben.
Who you wish you had talked to.
Asked questions.
About Cuba.
Leaving home at sixteen.
How he made a Self.
The Man on the Christmas card
he sends every year
sitting by his pool
with Dog and Wife
far from kugels and call girls
in the Arizona sun.

Edward Pomerantz

18

She's Iris,
your babysitter,
who sits on your bed
and takes her sweater off,
circles your finger around her nipples,
like the O's in your tracing book.
Sometimes,
her boyfriend comes over,
and they make sounds in the living-room.
Once,
they ask you to come out of your room
with your pillow,
make believe it's a girl,
and kiss it,
which makes them laugh and cheer you on
to squeeze and fondle it.
That's your sex life
until you start jerking off,
reading the "good parts" in dirty books,
listening,
when your parents think you're asleep,
for the opening of the night table drawer
where your father keeps the Trojans,
sitting with Howie in the RKO,
Lewie between us,
both with one fist around Lewie's shlong,
watching Abbott and Costello Meet The Wolfman,
munching on Almond Joys,
Baby Ruths.

19

Today,
they'd have a name for it,
therapy,
meds.
Back then,
it was just Myron
being Myron
throwing a fit.
Just Myron,
left back
when the rest of us skipped a grade.
Just Myron,
smashing his leg through a window.
Just Myron.
Dead at 30
from just a brain tumor.

20

He saves twine
and broken barbershop clippers.
He smells sour,
wipes his mouth with his sleeve,
teaches you the Hebrew alphabet
on the kitchen fire-escape,
sits patting your hand by your bedside
when you have a bad ear infection,
repeating "Don't cry. I cry. Don't cry. I cry."
This is all you remember
of your grandpa.
Your mother's father
who comes to live with us for a time.
Just aleph, bet, gimmel
over and over,
bits and pieces,
scraps,
what's left on the barber shop floor
after a haircut,
before the barber sweeps up.

21

She's waiting for you
at the bottom of the hill.
Waiting to hit you
for making her worry.
You're late.
If you're late
that can only mean something terrible has happened.
To not get hit,
you have to be hit by a truck,
dead in the gutter
or a hospital.
You're late today
because of the rainstorm.
The Principal won't let us leave
until it lets up.
And you can't get your rubbers on.
The backs of the rubbers won't give,
won't stretch
around the heels of your shoes,
your finger
keeps getting in the way.
It's still raining,
not so bad now.
You trudge down the hill
a boy soldier
facing the music.
She can't help herself, she says.
She knows it's crazy,
doesn't know what comes over her,
gets into her.

Her accomplice,
you'll let her do what she has to,
a couple of whacks on the head

and it's over,
your only shame
the sound of your rubbers,
as you come closer,
half on,
half off,
flapping.

22

Your mother tells your father
he needs to throw a ball,
play catch with you.
That's what fathers do.
It will bring the two of us closer.
Your father tells your mother
she's too close,
she's suffocating you.
Too close.
Not close enough.
At what distance
do you get it right?

Edward Pomerantz

23

He has a Chinese customer.
Comes in every year
for carp
for the holidays.
Your father welcomes this customer
with an open heart,
jokes and laughs with him,
throws in extra fish heads.
When the customer leaves,
your father goes back to scraping a porgy,
whistling.
"Let's eat out,"
he says later,
closing up.
"I'm in the mood for Chinx tonight."

24

"Fight me."

We're on a train to New Haven,
where we'll find an apartment for me
my first year at Graduate School.

I'm 22.
She's 41.
Only 19 when she gave birth to me,
a year after she married my father
the year her mother died
and she tried to leap into the grave after her,
screaming "Mama! Mama! Take me with you!"
her two brothers holding her back.

I grow up with that story,
love it for its "pure theatre,"
her bravura performance.

62, she takes an overdose of sleeping pills
and kills herself.
The books and articles tell you you're supposed to feel guilt
when someone you love decides the party's over.
If only you could have done something, etc.
Not me.
I know, as she knew, it was a long time coming.
She had an appointment to keep.
Like the song says:
"Mammy. Mammy. I'm comin'. So sorry that I made you wait.
Mammy. Mammy. I'm comin'! Oh God, I hope I'm not too late."

On the train, we're playing Gin.
If she didn't work in the store with my father,
she would have been a riverboat gambler,

puffing on her Camel,
shuffling and dealing,
the cards old friends.

No-one can beat her.
She remembers every card you pick up, discard.
She knows every card in your hand, the cards still in the deck.
If she can't outsmart death,
she'll be the winner
at Canasta, Mah Jong, Bridge.

"We have to talk."

It's the final round.
My hand full of possibilities.
She flicks a speck of tobacco from her tongue.

"Once you're out of the house, I'm out of your life. That won't
be easy. You know the trouble I have letting go. I hold on too
tight. My mother, may she rest, called me her mamele, her little
mother. To fill the hole she left, I made you my mamele, made
you my life."

The three of spades I discard is a card she's been waiting for.
She picks it up, slides it in place, discards a jack of diamonds.
I take a card from the deck.
She blows out smoke.

"Big mistake. Your father says we're too close. Too alike. And he's
right. You have to break away now, be yourself. You don't want
to follow me into the grave like I tried to follow my mother. You
have to promise… If I *can't* let go…If I'm too weak…If I *keep*
holding on…you'll *fight* me."

It's a moment outside of time.
Train rocking.

Her eyes, a tiger's, behind a fan of cards.
Mine staring back
at the pretty freckled young mother
from whose fatal grip I'd be forever wrestling
to free myself,
and at this moment, love fiercely.

"Gin," I tell her.

She looks down at the card
which somewhere before "You have to promise,"
she had tossed from her hand.

I pick it up,
end the game.

"Shit."
Crushing out her Camel, she lights the next one.
"I knew you had kings. That's what happens when you play and *talk*."

Edward Pomerantz

25

The orange velvet easy chair.
His.
Now yours.
The chair you're sitting in
when you stop the work you're doing,
look up,
decide to quit your job tomorrow.
You like this job.
You're good at it.
But you need more room,
more space.
You need to get out.
Into the world.

"Into the destructive element, immerse."

These are the words you hear,
speak aloud.
Joseph Conrad's words,
from Lord Jim,
read years ago
when you were a college boy,
coming back to you,
now,
in your dead father's chair.

Once,
years before,
when you took a walk along the Hudson together
and stood looking out at the shad nets,
your father said
"One thing. I can tell you. Always be happy in your work."

Is this why Conrad comes to you?

Speaks to you?
Why you quit your job?

"Always be happy in your work."
"Into the destructive element, immerse."

Same thing.

26

If my father was alive today
we'd be old men together.

Edward Pomerantz

About the Author

Edward Pomerantz is an award winning playwright,
screenwriter, novelist, filmmaker, and teacher. He wrote the
movie *Caught*, based on his novel *Into It*, a Sundance Centerpiece
Premiere, released by Sony Pictures Classics and nominated
for three Independent Spirit Awards. His plays have been
staged in New York, Los Angeles, and in Greece at the Athens
Fringe Festival. His novellas and short stories were published
by *Contact*, the *San Francisco Collection of New Writing, Art and
Ideas*, and *Ms Magazine*. His short films and screenplays have
won awards at international film festivals in Madrid, Calcutta,
Stockholm, Paris, and London. As a teacher, mentor, creative
advisor, and visiting writer, he has worked with over a thousand
writers on their novels, plays, and screenplays at various
universities, workshops, and theatre academies in Colorado, New
York, Mexico, Germany, Spain, England, Brazil, Poland, Russia,
and Cuba. He has written over 30 commissioned screenplays
and television scripts, and is the recipient of two Writers Guild
Awards and two Fulbright Specialist Grants. On the faculty
at SUNY-Purchase in the School of Film and Media Studies,
he also serves as the Director of the Harlem Dramatic Writing
Workshop, a free program of workshops created to find and
nurture gifted storytellers in the Harlem community.

The Jewish Poetry Project

jpoetry.us

Ben Yehuda Press

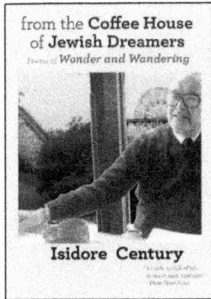

From the Coffee House of Jewish Dreamers: Poems of Wonder and Wandering and the Weekly Torah Portion by Isidore Century

"Isidore Century is a wonderful poet. His poems are funny, deeply observed, without pretension." – *The Jewish Week*

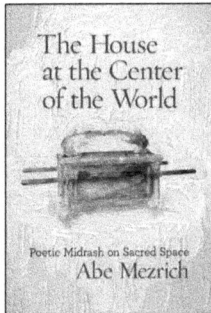

The House at the Center of the World: Poetic Midrash on Sacred Space by Abe Mezrich

"Direct and accessible, Mezrich's midrashic poems often tease profound meaning out of his chosen Torah texts. These poems remind us that our Creator is forgiving, that the spiritual and physical can inform one another, and that the supernatural can be carried into the everyday."
—Yehoshua November, author of *God's Optimism*

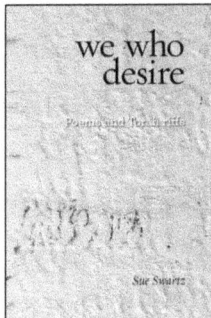

we who desire: Poems and Torah riffs by Sue Swartz

"Sue Swartz does magnificent acrobatics with the Torah. She takes the English that's become staid and boring, and adds something that's new and strange and exciting. These are poems that leave a taste in your mouth, and you walk away from them thinking, what did I just read? Oh, yeah. It's the Bible."
—Matthue Roth, author of *Yom Kippur A Go-Go*

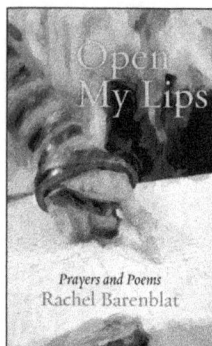

Open My Lips: Prayers and Poems
by Rachel Barenblat

"Barenblat's God is a personal God—one who lets her cry on His shoulder, and who rocks her like a colicky baby. These poems bridge the gap between the ineffable and the human. This collection will bring comfort to those with a religion of their own, as well as those seeking a relationship with some kind of higher power."
—Satya Robyn, author of *The Most Beautiful Thing*

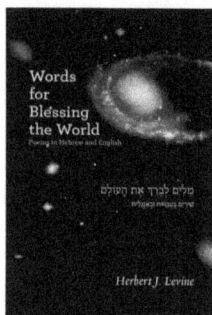

Words for Blessing the World: Poems in Hebrew and English by Herbert J. Levine

"These writings express a profoundly earth-based theology in a language that is clear and comprehensible. These are works to study and learn from."
—Rodger Kamenetz, author of *The Jew in the Lotus*

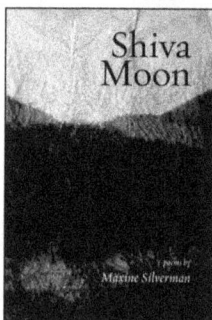

Shiva Moon: Poems by Maxine Silverman

"The poems, deeply felt, are spare, spoken in a quiet but compelling voice, as if we were listening in to her inner life. This book is a precious record of the transformation saying Kaddish can bring."
—Howard Schwartz, author of *The Library of Dreams*

is: heretical Jewish blessings and poems by Yaakov Moshe (Jay Michaelson)

"Finally, Torah that speaks to and through the lives we are actually living: expanding the tent of holiness to embrace what has been cast out, elevating what has been kept down, advancing what has been held back, reveling in questions, revealing contradictions."
—Eden Pearlstein, aka eprhyme

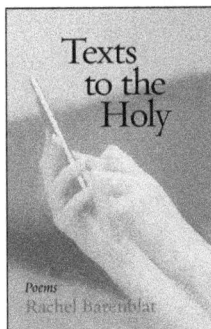

Texts to the Holy: Poems
by Rachel Barenblat

"These poems are remarkable, radiating a love of God that is full bodied, innocent, raw, pulsating, hot, drunk. I can hardly fathom their faith but am grateful for the vistas they open. I will sit with them, and invite you to do the same."
—Merle Feld, author of *A Spiritual Life*

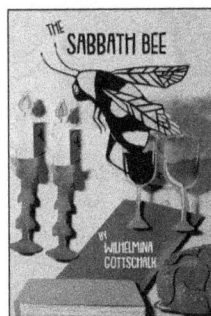

The Sabbath Bee: Love Songs to Shabbat
by Wilhelmina Gottschalk

"Torah, say our sages, has seventy faces. As these prose poems reveal, so too does Shabbat. Here we meet Shabbat as familiar housemate, as the child whose presence transforms a family, as a spreading tree, as an annoying friend who insists on being celebrated, as a woman, as a man, as a bee, as the ocean."
—Rachel Barenblat, author of *The Velveteen Rabbi's Haggadah*

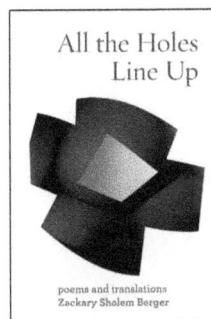

All the Holes Line Up: Poems and Translations
by Zackary Sholem Berger

"Spare and precise, Berger's poems gaze unflinchingly at—but also celebrate—human imperfection in its many forms. And what a delight that Berger also includes in this collection a handful of his resonant translations of some of the great Yiddish poets." —Yehoshua November, author of *God's Optimism* and *Two World Exist*

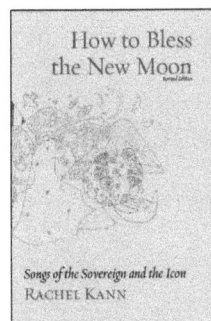

How to Bless the New Moon:
Songs of the Sovereign and the Icon
by Rachel Kann

"Rachel Kann is a master wordsmith. Her poems are rich in content, packed with life's wisdom and imbued with soul. May this collection of her work enable more of the world to enjoy her offerings."
—Sarah Yehudit Schneider, author of *You Are What You Hate* and *Kabbalistic Writings on the Nature of Masculine and Feminine*

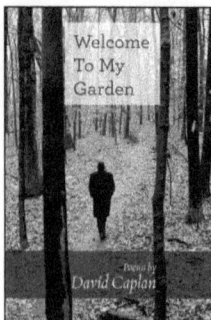

Into My Garden
by David Caplan

"The beauty of Caplan's book is that it is not polemical. It does not set out to win an argument or ask you whether you've put your tefillin on today. These gentle poems invite the reader into one person's profound, ambiguous religious experience."
—*The Jewish Review of Books*

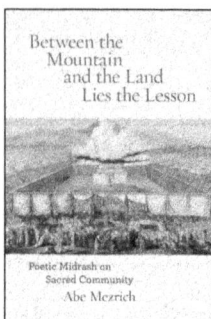

Between the Mountain and the Land is the Lesson: Poetic Midrash on Sacred Community
by Abe Mezrich

"Abe Mezrich cuts straight back to the roots of the Midrashic tradition, sermonizing as a poet, rather than idealogue. Best of all, Abe knows how to ask questions and avoid the obvious answers."
—Jake Marmer, author of *Jazz Talmud*

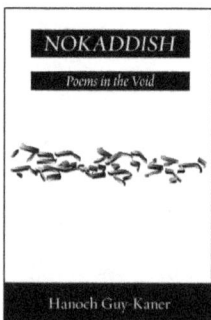

NOKADDISH: Poems in the Void
by Hanoch Guy Kaner

"A subversive, midrashic play with meanings–specifically Jewish meanings, and then the reversal and negation of these meanings."
—Robert G. Margolis

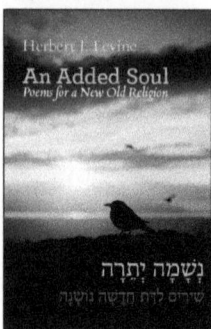

An Added Soul: Poems for a New Old Religion
by Herbert J. Levine

"These poems are remarkable, radiating a love of God that is full bodied, innocent, raw, pulsating, hot, drunk. I can hardly fathom their faith but am grateful for the vistas they open. I will sit with them, and invite you to do the same."
—Merle Feld, author of *A Spiritual Life*.

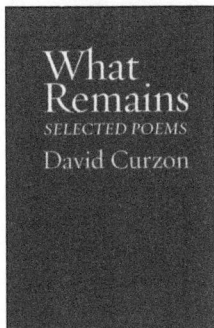

What Remains
by David Curzon

"Aphoristic, ekphrastic, and precise revelations animate WHAT REMAINS. In his stunning rewriting of Psalm 1 and other biblical passages, Curzon shows himself to be a fabricator, a collector, and an heir to the literature, arts, and wisdom traditions of the planet."
—Alicia Ostriker, author of *The Volcano and After*

The Shortest Skirt in Shul
by Sass Oron

"These poems exuberantly explore gender, Torah, the masks we wear, and the way our bodies (and the ways we wear them) at once threaten stable narratives, and offer the kind of liberation that saves our lives."
—Alicia Jo Rabins, author of *Divinity School*, composer of *Girls In Trouble*

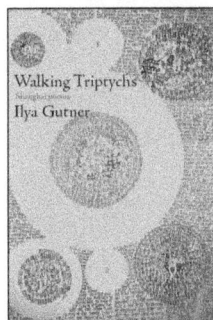

Walking Triptychs
by Ilya Gutner

These are poems from when I walked about Shanghai and thought about the meaning of the Holocaust.

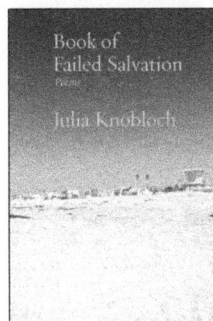

Book of Failed Salvation
by Julia Knobloch

"These beautiful poems express a tender longing for spiritual, physical, and emotional connection. They detail a life in movement—across distances, faith, love, and doubt."
—David Caplan, author of *Into My Garden*

Daily Blessings: Poems on Tractate Berakhot
by Hillel Broder

"Hillel Broder does not just write poetry about the Talmud; he also draws out the Talmud's poetry, finding lyricism amidst legality and re-setting the Talmud's rich images like precious gems in end-stopped lines of verse."
—Ilana Kurshan, author of *If All the Seas Were Ink*

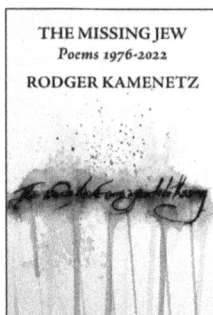

The Missing Jew: Poems 1976-2022
by Rodger Kamenetz

"How does Rodger Kamenetz manage to have so singular a voice and at the same time precisely encapsulate the world view of an entire generation (also mine) of text-hungry American Jews born in the middle of the twentieth century?"
—Jacqueline Osherow, author of *Ultimatum from Paradise* and *My Lookalike at the Krishna Temple: Poems*

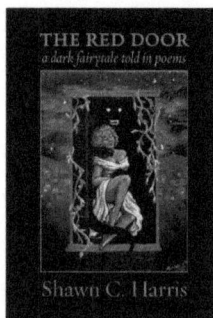

The Red Door: A dark fairy tale told in poems
by Shawn C. Harris

"THE RED DOOR, like its poet author Shawn C. Harris, transcends genres and identities. It is an exploration in crossing worlds. It brings together poetry and story telling, imagery and life events, spirit and body, the real and the fantastic, Jewish past and Jewish present, to spin one tale."
—Einat Wilf, author of *The War of Return*

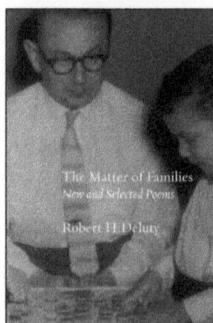

The Matter of Families
by Robert H. Deluty

"Robert Deluty's career-spanning collection of New and Selected poems captures the essence of his work: the power of love, joy, and connection, all tied together with the poet's glorious sense of humor. This book is Deluty's masterpiece."
—Richard M. Berlin, M.D., author of *Freud on My Couch*

The Five Books of Limericks
by Rhonda Rosenheck

The Five Books
of Limericks

A chapter by chapter retelling of the Torah

Rhonda
Rosenheck

"A biblical commentary that is truly unique. Each chapter of the Torah is distilled into its own limerick, leading the reader to reconsider the meaning of the original text, and opening avenues for interpretation that are both fun and insightful."
—Rabbi Hillel Norry

Bits and Pieces
by Edward Pomerantz

"A stunning tapestry of family life in the 40s and 50s. Like all great poetry, Pomerantz's work expands after reading. Each poem is exquisitely structured, often with a stunning ending, into a masterful whole."
—Alan Ziegler, editor of *SHORT: An International Anthology*

Words for a Dazzling Firmament: Poems/ Readings on Bereishit Through Shemot
by Abe Mezrich

"Mezrich is a cultivated craftsman— interpretively astute, sonically deliberate, and spiritually cunning."
—Zohar Atkins, author of *Nineveh*

Everything Thaws
by R. B. Lemberg

"Full of glacier-sharp truths, and moments revealed between words like bodies beneath melting permafrost. As it becomes increasingly plain how deeply our world is shaped by war and climate change and grief and anger, articulating that shape feels urgent and necessary and painful and healing."
—Ruthanna Emrys, author of *A Half-Built Garden*

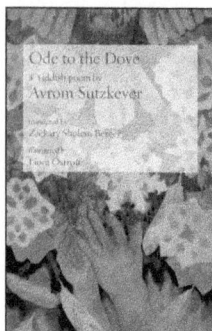

Ode to the Dove
An illustrated, bilingual edition of a Yiddish poem by Abraham Sutzkever
Zackary Sholem Berger, translator
Liora Ostroff, Illustrator

"An elegant volume for lovers of poetry."
—Justin Cammy, translator of *Sutzkever, From the Vilna Ghetto to Nuremberg: Memoir and Testimony*

Poems for a Cartoon Mouse
by Andrew Burt

"Andrew Burt's poetry magnifies the vanishingly small line between danger and safety. This collection asks whether order is an illusion that veils chaos, or vice-versa, juxtaposing images from the Bible with animated films."
—Ari Shapiro, host of NPR's *All Things Considered*

Old Shul
by Pinny Bulman

"Nostalgia gives way to a tender theology, a softly chuckling illumination from within the heart of/as a beautiful, broken sanctuary, somehow both gritty and fragile, grimy and iridescent – not unlike faith itself."
—Jake Marmer, author of *Cosmic Diaspora*

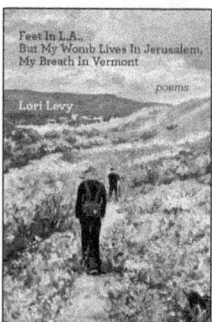

Feet In L.A., But My Womb Lives In Jerusalem, My Breath In Vermont
by Lori Levy

"Reading through Lori Levy's new book of poems takes my breath away. With no pretense whatsoever, they leap, alive, from the page until this reader felt as if she were living Levy's life. How does the author do it?"
—Mary Jo Balistreri, author of *Still*

www.ingramcontent.com/pod-product-compliance
Lightning Source LLC
Chambersburg PA
CBHW022041090426
42741CB00007B/1156